## CHANGING COLORS

Work the last stitch to within one step of completion, hook new yarn ***(Fig. 4)*** and draw through all loops on hook.

**Fig. 4**

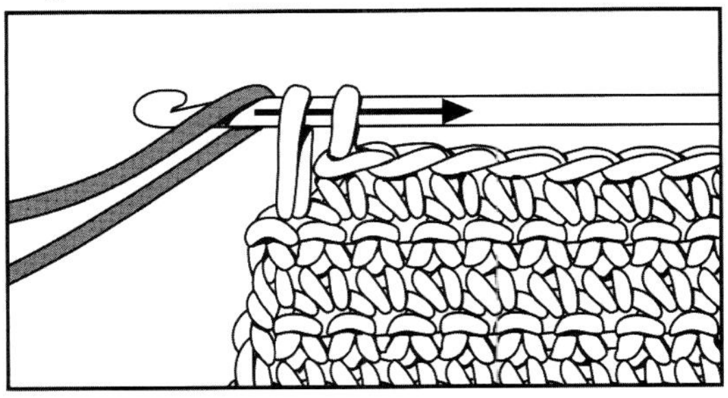

## FRINGE

Cut a piece of cardboard 5" wide and 8" long. Wind the yarn **loosely** and **evenly** around the cardboard lengthwise until the card is filled, then cut across one end; repeat as needed.
Hold together as many strands of yarn as specified in individual instructions; fold in half.
With **wrong** side facing and using a crochet hook, draw the folded end up through a row, stitch, or space and pull the loose ends through the folded end ***(Fig. 5a or 5c)***; draw the knot up **tightly** ***(Fig. 5b or 5d)***.
Lay flat on a hard surface and trim the ends.

**Fig. 5a**

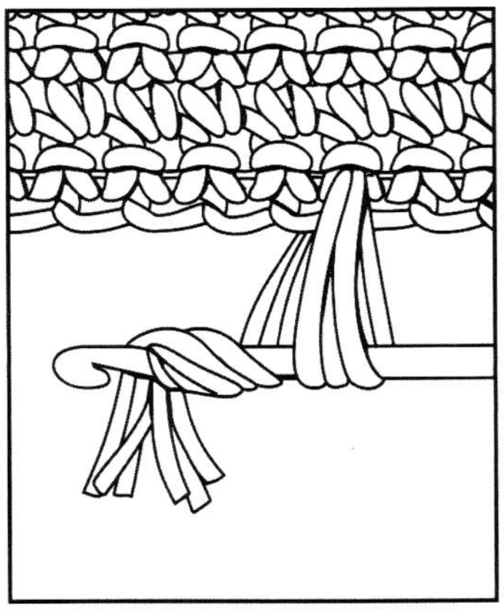

**Fig. 5b**

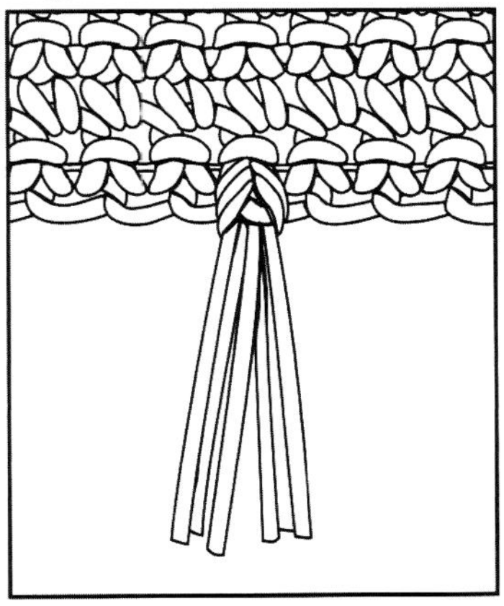

**Fig. 5c**

**Fig. 5d**

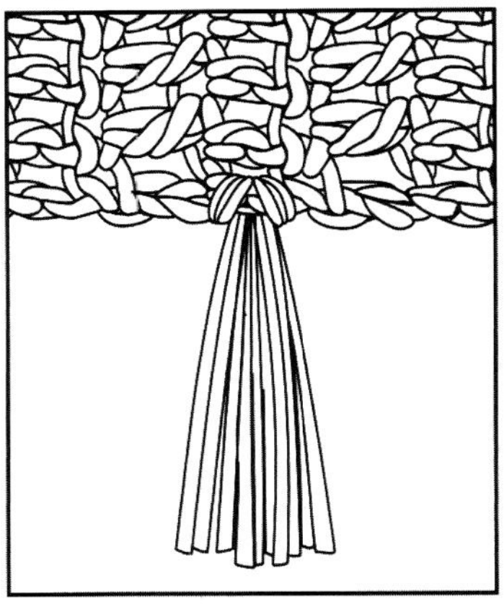

# 1. BABY BLUE

**Finished Size:** 36" x $45\frac{1}{2}$"

**MATERIALS**

Worsted Weight Yarn:
- Variegated - 19 ounces, (540 grams, 1,075 yards)
- Blue - 19 ounces, (540 grams, 1,075 yards)

Crochet hook, size P (10.00 mm) **or** size needed for gauge

***Note:*** Each row is worked across length of Afghan holding two strands of yarn together.

**GAUGE:** In pattern, 2 repeats = $2\frac{3}{4}$"; 4 rows = 3"

**Gauge Swatch:** $4\frac{1}{2}$"w x 4"h
Ch 12 **loosely**.
Work same as Afghan for 5 rows.
Finish off.

## AFGHAN

With one strand of Variegated and one strand of Blue, ch 102 **loosely**.

**Row 1** (Right side)**:** Dc in back ridge of fourth ch from hook ***(Fig. 1, page 1)*** and each ch across **(3 skipped chs count as first dc)**: 100 dc.

***Note:*** Loop a short piece of yarn around any stitch to mark Row 1 as **right** side.

**Row 2:** Ch 1, turn, sc in first dc, ★ ch 2, skip next 2 dc, sc in next dc; repeat from ★ across: 34 sc and 33 ch-2 sps.

**Row 3:** Ch 3 **(counts as first dc, now and throughout)**, turn; (2 dc in next ch-2 sp, dc in next sc) across: 100 dc.

**Row 4:** Ch 1, turn, sc in first dc, ★ ch 2, skip next 2 dc, sc in next dc; repeat from ★ across: 34 sc and 33 ch-2 sps.

**Row 5:** Ch 3, turn; (2 dc in next ch-2 sp, dc in next sc) across: 100 dc.

Repeat Rows 4 and 5 until Afghan measures approximately 36" from beginning ch, ending by working Row 5.

Finish off.

Holding 4 strands of Variegated and 4 strands of Blue together, add fringe in end of each right side row across short edges of Afghan ***(Figs. 5c & d)***.

7

4

# 2. PRETTY PASTELS

**Finished Size:** 36" x 46"

**MATERIALS**
Worsted Weight Yarn:
Variegated - $18^3/_4$ ounces, (530 grams, 1,060 yards)
White - $16^1/_2$ ounces, (470 grams, 930 yards)
Crochet hook, size P (10.00 mm) **or** size needed for gauge

*Note:* Afghan is worked holding two strands of yarn together.

**GAUGE:** In pattern, sc, (ch 1, sc) 4 times and 8 rows = $3^3/_4$"

**Gauge Swatch:** 4" square
Ch 10 **loosely**.
Work same as Afghan for 8 rows.
Finish off.

## AFGHAN

With one strand of Variegated and one strand of White, ch 88 **loosely**.

**Row 1** (Right side)**:** Sc in second ch from hook, ★ ch 1, skip next ch, sc in next ch; repeat from ★ across: 44 sc.

*Note:* Loop a short piece of yarn around any stitch to mark Row 1 as **right** side.

**Row 2:** Ch 1, turn; sc in first sc, (ch 1, sc in next sc) across.

Repeat Row 2 until Afghan measures approximately 46" from beginning ch, ending by working a **right** side row.

Finish off.

Holding 5 strands of Variegated together, add fringe in each ch-1 sp across short edges of Afghan ***(Figs. 5a & b, page 2)***.

# 3. PASTEL RIPPLE

**Finished Size:** 38" x $45^1/_2$"

**MATERIALS**
Worsted Weight Yarn:
White - $32^1/_2$ ounces, (920 grams, 1,835 yards)
Blue - 5 ounces, (140 grams, 285 yards)
Yellow - $3^1/_2$ ounces, (100 grams, 200 yards)
Crochet hook, size P (10.00 mm) **or** size needed for gauge

*Note:* Afghan is worked holding two strands of yarn together.

**GAUGE:** In pattern, from point to point = $6^1/_4$";
4 rows = $4^1/_4$"

**Gauge Swatch:** 13"w x $4^1/_2$"h
Ch 40 **loosely**.
Work same as Afghan for 4 rows.
Finish off.

To work **color change**, work the last dc to within one step of completion, cut one strand of yarn, hook new yarn and remaining strand and draw through both loops on hook ***(Fig. 4, page 2)***.

## AFGHAN

With one strand of White and one strand of Blue, ch 108 **loosely**.

**Row 1** (Right side)**:** 3 Dc in fifth ch from hook **(4 skipped chs count as first dc plus ch 1)**, (skip next 2 chs, 3 dc in next ch) twice, skip next 4 chs, (3 dc in next ch, skip next 2 chs) twice, ★ (3 dc, ch 2, 3 dc) in next ch, (skip next 2 chs, 3 dc in next ch) twice, skip next 4 chs, (3 dc in next ch, skip next 2 chs) twice; repeat from ★ 4 times **more**, 3 dc in next ch, ch 1, dc in last ch changing to two strands of White: 110 dc and 7 sps.

*Note:* Loop a short piece of yarn around any stitch to mark Row 1 as **right** side.

**Row 2:** Ch 4 **(counts as first dc plus ch 1, now and throughout)**, turn; 3 dc in next ch-1 sp, (skip next 2 dc, 3 dc in next dc) twice, skip next 5 dc, 3 dc in next dc, skip next 2 dc, 3 dc in next dc, ★ (3 dc, ch 2, 3 dc) in next ch-2 sp, (skip next 2 dc, 3 dc in next dc) twice, skip next 5 dc, 3 dc in next dc, skip next 2 dc, 3 dc in next dc; repeat from ★ 4 times **more**, 3 dc in next ch-1 sp, ch 1, dc in last dc.

**Row 3:** Ch 4, turn; 3 dc in next ch-1 sp, (skip next 2 dc, 3 dc in next dc) twice, skip next 5 dc, 3 dc in next dc, skip next 2 dc, 3 dc in next dc, ★ (3 dc, ch 2, 3 dc) in next ch-2 sp, (skip next 2 dc, 3 dc in next dc) twice, skip next 5 dc, 3 dc in next dc, skip next 2 dc, 3 dc in next dc; repeat from ★ 4 times **more**, 3 dc in next ch-1 sp, ch 1, dc in last dc changing to one strand of White and one strand of Yellow.

**Row 4:** Ch 4, turn; 3 dc in next ch-1 sp, (skip next 2 dc, 3 dc in next dc) twice, skip next 5 dc, 3 dc in next dc, skip next 2 dc, 3 dc in next dc, ★ (3 dc, ch 2, 3 dc) in next ch-2 sp, (skip next 2 dc, 3 dc in next dc) twice, skip next 5 dc, 3 dc in next dc, skip next 2 dc, 3 dc in next dc; repeat from ★ 4 times **more**, 3 dc in next ch-1 sp, ch 1, dc in last dc changing to two strands of White.

**Row 5:** Ch 4, turn; 3 dc in next ch-1 sp, (skip next 2 dc, 3 dc in next dc) twice, skip next 5 dc, 3 dc in next dc, skip next 2 dc, 3 dc in next dc, ★ (3 dc, ch 2, 3 dc) in next ch-2 sp, (skip next 2 dc, 3 dc in next dc) twice, skip next 5 dc, 3 dc in next dc, skip next 2 dc, 3 dc in next dc; repeat from ★ 4 times **more**, 3 dc in next ch-1 sp, ch 1, dc in last dc.

**Row 6:** Ch 4, turn; 3 dc in next ch-1 sp, (skip next 2 dc, 3 dc in next dc) twice, skip next 5 dc, 3 dc in next dc, skip next 2 dc, 3 dc in next dc, ★ (3 dc, ch 2, 3 dc) in next ch-2 sp, (skip next 2 dc, 3 dc in next dc) twice, skip next 5 dc, 3 dc in next dc, skip next 2 dc, 3 dc in next dc; repeat from ★ 4 times **more**, 3 dc in next ch-1 sp, ch 1, dc in last dc changing to one strand of White and one strand of Blue.

**Row 7:** Ch 4, turn; 3 dc in next ch-1 sp, (skip next 2 dc, 3 dc in next dc) twice, skip next 5 dc, 3 dc in next dc, skip next 2 dc, 3 dc in next dc, ★ (3 dc, ch 2, 3 dc) in next ch-2 sp, (skip next 2 dc, 3 dc in next dc) twice, skip next 5 dc, 3 dc in next dc, skip next 2 dc, 3 dc in next dc; repeat from ★ 4 times **more**, 3 dc in next ch-1 sp, ch 1, dc in last dc changing to two strands of White.

**Rows 8-42:** Repeat Rows 2-7, 5 times; then repeat Rows 2-6 once **more**.

**Row 43:** Ch 4, turn; 3 dc in next ch-1 sp, (skip next 2 dc, 3 dc in next dc) twice, skip next 5 dc, 3 dc in next dc, skip next 2 dc, 3 dc in next dc, ★ (3 dc, ch 2, 3 dc) in next ch-2 sp, (skip next 2 dc, 3 dc in next dc) twice, skip next 5 dc, 3 dc in next dc, skip next 2 dc, 3 dc in next dc; repeat from ★ 4 times **more**, 3 dc in next ch-1 sp, ch 1, dc in last dc; finish off.

Holding 5 strands of White and 5 strands of Blue together, add fringe in each point across short edges of Afghan *(Figs. 5a & b, page 2)*.

6

2

# 4. ROCK-A-BYE RIPPLE

**Finished Size:** 36" x 51"

**MATERIALS**

Worsted Weight Yarn:
- White - 26 ounces, (740 grams, 1,470 yards)
- Blue - 10½ ounces, (300 grams, 595 yards)
- Pink - 5½ ounces, (160 grams, 310 yards)

Crochet hook, size P (10.00 mm) **or** size needed for gauge

***Note:*** Afghan is worked holding two strands of yarn together.

**GAUGE:** In pattern, 2 repeats = 4¼";
6 rows = 3¼"

**Gauge Swatch:** 4½"w x 3½"h
Ch 13 **loosely**.
Work same as Afghan for 6 rows.
Finish off.

To work **color change**, work the last sc to within one step of completion, cut one strand of yarn, hook new yarn and remaining strand and draw through both loops on hook ***(Fig. 4, page 2)***.

## AFGHAN

With one strand of White and one strand of Blue, ch 118 **loosely**.

**Row 1:** Working in back ridges of beginning ch ***(Fig. 1, page 1)***, sc in second ch from hook and in next ch, 3 sc in next ch, sc in next 2 chs, ★ skip next 2 chs, sc in next 2 chs, 3 sc in next ch, sc in next 2 chs; repeat from ★ across: 119 sc.

**Row 2** (Right side)**:** Ch 1, turn; sc in first sc, skip next sc, working in Back Loops Only ***(Fig. 2, page 1)***, sc in next sc, 3 sc in next sc, ★ sc in next 2 sc, skip next 2 sc, sc in next 2 sc, 3 sc in next sc; repeat from ★ across to last 3 sc, sc in next sc, skip next sc, sc in **both** loops of last sc changing to one strand of White and one strand of Pink.

**Row 3:** Ch 1, turn; sc in both loops of first sc, skip next sc, working in Back Loops Only, sc in next sc, 3 sc in next sc, ★ sc in next 2 sc, skip next 2 sc, sc in next 2 sc, 3 sc in next sc; repeat from ★ across to last 3 sc, sc in next sc, skip next sc, sc in **both** loops of last sc.

**Row 4:** Ch 1, turn; sc in both loops of first sc, skip next sc, working in Back Loops Only, sc in next sc, 3 sc in next sc, ★ sc in next 2 sc, skip next 2 sc, sc in next 2 sc, 3 sc in next sc; repeat from ★ across to last 3 sc, sc in next sc, skip next sc, sc in **both** loops of last sc changing to one strand of White and one strand of Blue.

**Rows 5 and 6:** Repeat Rows 3 and 4 changing to two strands of White at end of last row.

**Rows 7 and 8:** Repeat Rows 3 and 4 changing to one strand of White and one strand of Blue at end of last row.

**Rows 9 and 10:** Repeat Rows 3 and 4 changing to one strand of White and one strand of Pink at end of last row.

**Rows 11-93:** Repeat Rows 3-10, 10 times; then repeat Rows 3-5 once **more**.

**Row 94:** Ch 1, turn; sc in both loops of first sc, skip next sc, working in Back Loops Only, sc in next sc, 3 sc in next sc, ★ sc in next 2 sc, skip next 2 sc, sc in next 2 sc, 3 sc in next sc; repeat from ★ across to last 3 sc, sc in next sc, skip next sc, sc in **both** loops of last sc; finish off.

# 5. SWEET DREAMS

**Finished Size:** 39½" x 49"

**MATERIALS**

Worsted Weight Yarn:
- White - 25½ ounces, (720 grams, 1,440 yards)
- Aqua - 5½ ounces, (160 grams, 310 yards)
- Pink - 5 ounces, (140 grams, 285 yards)
- Green - 5 ounces, (140 grams, 285 yards)
- Blue - 5 ounces, (140 grams, 285 yards)
- Yellow - 5 ounces, (140 grams, 285 yards)

Crochet hook, size P (10.00 mm) **or** size needed for gauge

*Note:* Each row is worked across length of Afghan holding two strands of yarn together. When joining yarn and finishing off, leave a 7" end to be worked into fringe.

**GAUGE:** In pattern, 8 dc = 4"; 4 rows = 3"

**Gauge Swatch:** 4"w x 3¾"h
Ch 9 **loosely**.
Work same as Afghan for 5 rows.

## AFGHAN

With one strand of White and one strand of Aqua, ch 99 **loosely**.

**Row 1** (Right side)**:** Sc in back ridge of second ch from hook *(Fig. 1, page 1)* and each ch across: 98 sc.

*Note:* Loop a short piece of yarn around any stitch to mark Row 1 as **right** side.

**Row 2:** Ch 3 **(counts as first dc)**, turn; 2 dc in next sc, (skip next sc, 2 dc in next sc) across to last 2 sc, skip next sc, dc in last sc; finish off.

**Row 3:** With **right** side facing, using one strand of White and one strand of Pink, join yarn with dc in first dc ***(see Joining With Dc, page 1)***; skip next dc, 2 dc in sp **before** next dc, (skip next 2 dc, 2 dc in sp **before** next dc) across to last 2 dc, skip next dc, dc in last dc; finish off.

**Row 4:** With **wrong** side facing, using one strand of White and one strand of Green, join yarn with dc in first dc; skip next dc, 2 dc in sp **before** next dc, (skip next 2 dc, 2 dc in sp **before** next dc) across to last 2 dc, skip next dc, dc in last dc; finish off.

**Row 5:** With one strand of White and one strand of Blue, repeat Row 3.

**Row 6:** With one strand of White and one strand of Yellow, repeat Row 4.

**Row 7:** With one strand of White and one strand of Aqua, repeat Row 3.

**Row 8:** With one strand of White and one strand of Pink, repeat Row 4.

**Row 9:** With one strand of White and one strand of Green, repeat Row 3.

**Row 10:** With one strand of White and one strand of Blue, repeat Row 4.

**Row 11:** With one strand of White and one strand of Yellow, repeat Row 3.

**Row 12:** With one strand of White and one strand of Aqua, repeat Row 4.

**Rows 13-52:** Repeat Rows 3-12, 4 times; at end of Row 52, do **not** finish off.

**Row 53:** Ch 1, turn; sc in each dc across; finish off.

Holding 2 strands of White and 2 strands of corresponding color yarn together, add additional fringe in end of each row ***(Figs. 5c & d, page 2)***.

# 6. COZY CUDDLE

**Finished Size:** 35" x 48"

**MATERIALS**

Worsted Weight Yarn:
Variegated - 17½ ounces, (500 grams, 990 yards)
Green - 17½ ounces, (500 grams, 990 yards)
Crochet hook, size P (10.00 mm) **or** size needed for gauge

*Note:* Afghan is worked holding two strands of yarn together.

**GAUGE:** In pattern, one repeat = 2½"; 4 rows = 4¼"

**Gauge Swatch:** 5¼"w x 4½"h
Ch 15 **loosely**.
Work same as Afghan for 4 rows.
Finish off.

## AFGHAN

With one strand of Variegated and one strand of Green, ch 87 **loosely**.

**Row 1** (Right side)**:** 5 Dc in sixth ch from hook, skip next 2 chs, dc in next ch, ★ skip next 2 chs, 5 dc in next ch, skip next 2 chs, dc in next ch; repeat from ★ across: 84 dc.

*Note:* Loop a short piece of yarn around any stitch to mark Row 1 as **right** side.

**Row 2:** Ch 3 **(counts as first dc, now and throughout)**, turn; skip next 2 dc, 5 dc in next dc, ★ skip next 2 dc, dc in next dc, skip next 2 dc, 5 dc in next dc; repeat from ★ across to last 2 dc, skip last 2 dc, dc in next ch: 85 dc.

**Row 3:** Ch 3, turn; ★ skip next 2 dc, 5 dc in next dc, skip next 2 dc, dc in next dc; repeat from ★ across.

Repeat Row 3 until Afghan measures approximately 48" from beginning ch, ending by working a **right** side row.

Finish off.

Holding 4 strands of Variegated and 4 strands of Green together, add fringe in center of each 5-dc group across short edges of Afghan *(Figs. 5a & b, page 2)*.

# 7. SUGAR & SPICE

**Finished Size:** 36" x 45"

**MATERIALS**

Worsted Weight Yarn:
Variegated - 21½ ounces, (610 grams, 1,215 yards)
Pink - 21½ ounces, (610 grams, 1,215 yards)
Crochet hook, size P (10.00 mm) **or** size needed for gauge

*Note:* Each row is worked across length of Afghan holding two strands of yarn together.

**GAUGE:** In pattern, 3 repeats = 5"; 6 rows = 4"

**Gauge Swatch:** 5½"w x 4¼"h
Ch 13 **loosely**.
Work same as Afghan for 6 rows.
Finish off.

## AFGHAN

With one strand of Variegated and one strand of Pink, ch 109 **loosely**.

**Row 1** (Right side)**:** Working in back ridges of beginning ch *(Fig. 1, page 1)*, 2 dc in third ch from hook, ★ skip next ch, slip st in next ch, skip next ch, 3 dc in next ch; repeat from ★ across to last 2 chs, skip next ch, sc in last ch: 107 sts.

**Row 2:** Ch 2, turn; 2 dc in first sc, skip next dc, slip st in next dc, ★ 3 dc in next dc, skip next 2 sts, slip st in next dc; repeat from ★ across, sc in next ch: 108 sts.

**Row 3:** Ch 2, turn; 2 dc in first sc, skip next 2 sts, slip st in next dc, ★ 3 dc in next dc, skip next 2 sts, slip st in next dc; repeat from ★ across, sc in top of beginning ch-2.

Repeat Row 3 until Afghan measures approximately 36" from beginning ch, ending by working a **right** side row.

Finish off.

3

9

# 8. RAINBOW STRIPES

**Finished Size:** 43$\frac{1}{2}$" x 52"

### MATERIALS

Worsted Weight Yarn:
- White - 30 ounces, (850 grams, 1,695 yards)
- Green - 5$\frac{1}{2}$ ounces, (160 grams, 310 yards)
- Blue - 4$\frac{1}{2}$ ounces, (130 grams, 250 yards)
- Yellow - 4$\frac{1}{2}$ ounces, (130 grams, 250 yards)
- Aqua - 4$\frac{1}{2}$ ounces, (130 grams, 250 yards)
- Pink - 4$\frac{1}{2}$ ounces, (130 grams, 250 yards)

Crochet hook, size P (10.00 mm) **or** size needed for gauge

*Note:* Each row is worked across length of Afghan holding two strands of yarn together. When joining yarn and finishing off, leave a 7" end to be worked into fringe.

**GAUGE:** 4 Cross Sts = 3$\frac{3}{4}$"; 6 rows = 4"

**Gauge Swatch:** 3$\frac{3}{4}$"w x 4$\frac{1}{4}$"h
Ch 9 **loosely**.
Work same as Afghan for 6 rows.

### STITCH GUIDE

**CROSS STITCH** ***(abbreviated Cross St)***
Skip next sc, dc in next sc, working **around** dc just made, dc in skipped sc.

## AFGHAN

With two strands of White, ch 113 **loosely**.

**Row 1** (Right side)**:** Sc in back ridge of second ch from hook ***(Fig. 1, page 1)*** and each ch across; finish off: 112 sc.

*Note:* Loop a short piece of yarn around any stitch to mark Row 1 as **right** side.

**Row 2:** With **wrong** side facing, using one strand of Green and one strand of White, join yarn with dc in first sc ***(see Joining With Dc, page 1)***; work Cross Sts across to last sc, dc in last sc; finish off: 55 Cross Sts.

**Row 3:** With **right** side facing, using one strand of Green and one strand of White, join yarn with sc in first dc ***(see Joining With Sc, page 1)***; sc in each dc across; finish off: 112 sc.

**Row 4:** With **wrong** side facing, using one strand of Green and one strand of White, join yarn with dc in first sc; work Cross Sts across to last sc, dc in last sc; finish off: 55 Cross Sts.

**Row 5:** With **right** side facing and using two strands of White, join yarn with sc in first dc; sc in each dc across; finish off: 112 sc.

**Rows 6-8:** With one strand of Blue and one strand of White, repeat Rows 2-4.

**Row 9:** Repeat Row 5.

**Rows 10-12:** With one strand of Yellow and one strand of White, repeat Rows 2-4.

**Row 13:** Repeat Row 5.

**Rows 14-16:** With one strand of Aqua and one strand of White, repeat Rows 2-4.

**Row 17:** Repeat Row 5.

**Rows 18-20:** With one strand of Pink and one strand of White, repeat Rows 2-4.

**Row 21:** Repeat Row 5.

**Rows 22-65:** Repeat Rows 2-21 twice, then repeat Rows 2-5 once **more**.

Holding a total of 6 strands of corresponding color yarn together, add additional fringe in end of right side rows ***(Figs. 5c & d, page 2)***.

# 9. SASSY STRIPES

**Finished Size:** 34$\frac{1}{2}$" x 45"

### MATERIALS

Worsted Weight Yarn:
- Variegated - 21$\frac{1}{2}$ ounces, (610 grams, 1,215 yards)
- Green - 9$\frac{1}{2}$ ounces, (270 grams, 535 yards)

Crochet hook, size P (10.00 mm) **or** size needed for gauge

*Note:* Each row is worked across length of Afghan holding two strands of yarn together.

**GAUGE:** In pattern, (Cluster, ch 1) 4 times and 4 rows = 3$\frac{3}{4}$"

**Gauge Swatch:** 4$\frac{1}{4}$"w x 4"h
Ch 13 **loosely**.
Work same as Afghan for 4 rows.